First World War
and Army of Occupation
War Diary
France, Belgium and Germany

28 DIVISION
84 Infantry Brigade
Northumberland Fusiliers
2nd Battalion
16 January 1915 - 31 October 1915

WO95/2277/2

The Naval & Military Press Ltd
www.nmarchive.com
Published in association with The National Archives

Published by

The Naval & Military Press Ltd

Unit 10 Ridgewood Industrial Park,

Uckfield, East Sussex,

TN22 5QE England

Tel: +44 (0) 1825 749494

www.naval-military-press.com

www.nmarchive.com

This diary has been reprinted in facsimile from the original. Any imperfections are inevitably reproduced and the quality may fall short of modern type and cartographic standards.

© Crown Copyright
Images reproduced by permission of The National Archives, London, England, 2015.

Contents

Document type	Place/Title	Date From	Date To
Heading	2nd Battalion Northumberland Fusiliers January 1915-October 1915		
Heading	28th Division 84th Infy Bde 2nd Bn Northumberland Fus. Jan-Oct 1915 To Salonikd		
Heading	28th Division. 84th Brigade. War Diary 2nd Northumberland Fusiliers 16th 31st January 1915		
War Diary		16/01/1915	31/01/1915
Heading	28th Division. 84th Brigade. War Diary 2nd Northumberland Fusiliers February 1915		
War Diary		01/02/1915	28/02/1915
Heading	War Diary 2nd Northumberland Fusiliers. March 1915		
War Diary		01/03/1915	31/03/1915
Heading	28th Division. 84th Infantry Brigade War Diary 2nd Northumberland Fusiliers April 1915		
War Diary		01/04/1915	30/04/1915
Heading	28th Division. 84th Inf. Bde. War Diary 2nd Northumberland Fusiliers 1st To 31st May 1915		
War Diary		01/05/1915	31/05/1915
Heading	84th Bde. 28th Division 2nd Northumberland Fusiliers. June 1915		
War Diary		01/06/1915	30/06/1915
Heading	84th Bde. 28th Div. 2nd Northumberland Fusiliers July 1915		
War Diary		01/07/1915	31/07/1915
Heading	84th Bde. 28th Div. 2nd Northumberland Fusiliers. August 1915		
Miscellaneous	On His Majesty's Service.		
War Diary		01/08/1915	31/08/1915
Heading	84th Bde. 28th Div. 2nd Northumberland Fusiliers September 1915		
Miscellaneous	On His Majesty's Service.		
War Diary		01/09/1915	30/09/1915
Heading	84th Bde. 29th Div. 20th Battalion Embarked For Salonika 23.10.15 2nd Northumberland Fusiliers. October 1915		
Miscellaneous	On His Majesty's Service.		
War Diary		01/10/1915	31/10/1915

2nd Battalion Northumberland Fusiliers
January 1915 – October 1915

28TH DIVISION
84TH INFY BDE

2ND BN NORTHUMBERLAND FUS.
JAN - OCT 1915

To SALONIKA

28th Division.
84th Brigade.

WAR DIARY

2nd NORTHUMBERLAND FUSILIERS

16th – 31st January

1915

2nd Bn. Northumberland Fusiliers 1

Hour date and place	Summary of events & Information	Remarks & references to appendices
12:43 pm 16-1-15	An advanced party of 1 officer and 5 N.C.O.s and men left WINCHESTER for overseas to arrange billets for the Battⁿ	
8.15 am 17-1-15	The Battⁿ paraded for Active Service and proceeded by march route to SOUTHAMPTON where it embarked on board S.S. AUSTRALIND strength 25 officers and 970 N.C.O.s and men after putting out from SOUTHAMPTON the ship lay off the Isle of WIGHT for the night	
11. am 18-1-15	The Battⁿ landed at HAVRE and entrained about 9.30pm	
5.30pm 19-1-15	The Battⁿ Detrained at HAZEBROUCK and marched to billets about 2 miles W of STRAZEELE	

Hour date and place	Summary of events Information	Remarks & references to appendices
20th and 21st	The Battⁿ settled into its billets in 13 farm houses round and about COURTE CROIX near STRAZEELE	
9.30am 22nd	The Battⁿ went for a route march. Several Aeroplanes were seen in the course of the march. A good deal of heavy firing was heard in the distance	
9.30am 23rd	The Battⁿ went for a route march. COURTE CROIX — METEREN — MERRIS — OUTERSTEENE back to COURTE CROIX.	
24th 10am	Church Parade: Major Moulton-Barrett spent the night in the trenches with 27th Division	
25th 9.30am to 1.30pm	Practised intrenching	

Hour date and place	Summary of events & Information	Remarks & reference to appendices
26th/1	Route march and night digging. L' Col. Endersby spent the night in the trenches with 27th Div.	
27th	Practised entrenching in proximity of billets	
28th	The Brigade was inspected in STAZEELE by Field Marshall Sir John French commanding in Chief. Capt Hart spent the night in the trenches with 27th Division	
29th	Route march and night digging	
30th	Practised digging by Day and relief of trenches by night	
31st	Church Parade in STAZEELE 1 officer and 1 N C O per Coy and the Signalling Sergt proceeded to YPRES to see the French Trenches which Battn is to take over on Feb 2nd	

28th Division.
84th Brigade.

WAR DIARY

2nd NORTHUMBERLAND FUSILIERS

February

1915

Hour, date and place.	Summary of events and Information	Remarks and References to appendices.
1st Feb 7.30 pm	The first line transport, supply and blanket waggons and officers chargers paraded to march to VLAMERTINGHE under Brigade arrangements	
2nd Feb 1.15 pm	The Battn marched to ROUGE CROIX [a distance of 1½ miles from its HdQrs where it] embarked in 38 motor buses which conveyed it to VLAMERTINGHE [at which place teas were issued, also one days rations and extra ammunition]. The Bn then marched thro' YPRES and ZILLEBEKE and relieved the 95th Regt of French Infantry in the front trenches occupying a line of about 1140 yds in extent. This line ran nearly due East and West and was situated about 800 yds from the south end	

Date & place	Summary of events and Information	Remarks and References to appendices
	of ZILLEBEKE Village, to our right trenches extending Eastwards about 1140 yds to our left trenches] The 7th Cavalry Brigade were in the trenches on our left, the 2nd Cheshire Regiment on our right and the 1/Welsh Regiment in support at TUILERIE just North of ZILLEBEKE and also at U Group trenches 500yds south of ZILLEBEKE. The trenches as taken over from the French were found to require a good deal of work to make them a strong line of defence the parapets in nearly all cases were hardly bullet proof; the trenches themselves especially those occupied by B and C Companies, being very wet and requiring draining. Owing to the non-arrival of picks and shovels this could not be taken in hand the 1st night. The companies occupied	

Hour, date and place	Summary of events and information	Remarks and references to appendices
	the trenches from right to left in the order A, B, C, D Companies. The four machine guns were in the front trenches.	
3rd Feb	Desultory firing had continued on both sides throughout the night. About 11 am on the 3rd the German artillery shelled the trenches B Company whose trenches formed a somewhat dangerous salient suffering most. Lt H.M. Heyder and 2Lt Montrohead were wounded and the machine gun with B Coy was damaged by shell fire. The German front trenches were distant from ours 150 yards in some cases to 30 yards in others.	
4th Feb	On the evening of the 4th the Ipswich Regt relieved the 13th in the front trenches	

Hour, date and place	Summary of events and information	Remarks and references to appendices
	and we went back to TUILERIE and U Trenches in support. The casualties during the time we were in the front trenches being 2 officers wounded. Other ranks 6 killed and 27 wounded. Owing to the Brigade on our right having lost some trenches and consequently having to deliver a counter attack on the night of the 4th/5th the relief was carried out very late and it was found impossible for the 1/Welch Regt to relieve all our line, consequently D Coy on our right remained in the front trenches, and were not relieved till the night of the 5th/6th.	
5th Feb.	The Battn remained in support, being shelled both in the morning and evening. There were however no casualties.	

Hour, date and place	Summary of events and information	Remarks and references to appendices
	about 6 p.m. on the evening of the 5th heavy firing broke out and the Battn was ordered to send two Companies and Battn Head Quarters to BLAUER POORT in support of the Suffolk Regiment. On arrival at BLAUER Poort however the situation had cleared and the two companies (A and B) returned to Headquarters. These companies having taken rations and material out to the 1/Welch Regt in the front trenches marched to YPRES where they remained for the night in the Infantry Barracks. The Bn HdQrs however and C and D companies remained at TUILERIE, two platoons of C being in U Trenches	

9

Hour, date and place	Summary of events and information	Remarks and references to appendix
6th	The Battⁿ relieved the 1st Welch in the front trenches. The companies being distributed as follows from right to left, C D A B. The night of the 6th/7th passed quietly.	
7th	There was a great deal of artillery fire on both sides during the 7th and	
8th	8th our casualties however for the two days amounted only to 1 killed and 7 wounded. The 1st Welch Regt relieved us on the evening of the 8th/9th. C and D companies marched to the Infantry Barracks YPRES. A and B companies and Bn Hd Qrs remaining at TUILERIE two platoons of A being in U Group Trenches.	
9th	The Battⁿ remained in support of the Welch Regiment as above	

Hour, date and place	Summary of events and information	Remarks and references to appendix
10th	On the night of the 10th/11th we again relieved the Welch Regiment being ourselves relieved on the night of the 11/12th by the 1st Bn East Yorkshire Regt our casualties for this period were 2/Lt Corbet Singleton wounded and other ranks 3 killed and 4 wounded	
11th	On the night of the 11/12th the Bn marched into billets via YPRES and VLAMERTINGE to a farm house two miles SW of the latter place where Bn HQ's were established. The men were partially in the farm buildings and partially in shelters — a sort of tarred canvas, V shaped Hut. Casualties up to date 3 officers wounded other ranks 10 killed 61 wounded	

Hour, date and place	Summary of events and information	Remarks and references to appendices
12th Feb	Bn was in billets [in huts and farm buildings near VLAMERTINGHE. Wooden huts were only half completed and leaked a good deal]	
13th Feb	Bn remained in billets [as on previous day and owing to bad weather nothing beyond cleaning up clothing and equipment could be carried out]	
14th Feb	Bn in same billets, Coys were sent in turn to a farm about 1½ miles away to bathe, dry clothes and change underclothing, 'D' Coy were unable to do this as Bn were called on & at 1 pm and marched to YPRES via VLAMERTINGHE. On reaching YPRES Coys moved up the Railway by platoons to TROIS ROIS and afterwards moved in to support trenches ½ mile S of CANAL and about 7 pm moved in to the dug outs in cutting	

Hour, date and place	Summary of events and information	Remarks and references to appendices
15th Feb	on CANAL BANK where they remained for the night. Bn spent the day on the CANAL BANK which was shelled about 1 p.m and four men of "A" Coy were wounded. After dark two Coys A&B moved back in two CHATEAU ROSENDAL and C&D Coys were sent up in support of an attack by the "Buffs" and E. SURREY REGT. and came under heavy shell fire in the open, and were eventually ordered to retire, and reached CHATEAU ROSENDAL in the early morning. Lt. Colonel Westerly was wounded during this attack.	
16th Feb	Day was spent in CHATEAU and Clark Bn was ordered to attack O.trench if the attack on P trench succeeded. Three Coys A, B & D marched to the point of deployment and lay down and awaited the attack on P. trench.	

Hour, date and place	Summary of events and information	Remarks and references to appendices
	this attack was not successful so the Bn withdrew coming under unaimed shell and maxim gun fire, Captain Auld being wounded. Two Coys C & D went to CANAL BANK, and A & B to CHATEAU	
17th Feb	On the evening of the 17th Bn moved up to the trenches and took over from the SUFFOLK Regt trenches situated N. of CANAL BANK.	
18th Feb	Bn was in trenches, in the evening part of M trench was taken over by the Argyll & Sutherland Highlanders. "B" Coy were relieved by D in N trench owing to the bad condition of the trench. Coys not in trenches on Canal Bank in support. 2 Coys 1st Bn North'n Fus came up during night to cover a working party of R.E and also the ground opposite O trench. Lt Pembroke was wounded during the night.	
19th Feb	Bn remained in trenches during the day and	

Hour, date and place	Summary of events and information	Remarks and references to appendices
	at night were relieved by the SUFFOLK Regt and moved back in to billets at KRUISSTAAT.	
20th Feb.	Arrived in billets at KRUISSTAAT at 5 a.m. Bn billeted in houses on each side of street. At 4 pm Bn was called out and ordered to proceed to LA CHAPELLE FARM and on reaching this point were moved up in to a large wood. At 11.15 pm orders were received to attack two lost trenches in conjunction with the CHESHIRE Regt. First attack consisting of 60 men of A Coy, 60 men of C Coy, 60 men of D Coy in three lines moved through a thick wood and came to an abattis in front of the trench they were attacking and on getting through this and attempting to charge were practically wiped out. Lts Legard Brownlow & Jenkins being wounded. A second attack ordered for an	

Hour, date and place	Summary of events and information	Remarks and references to appendices
	consisting of "B" Coy and details of "D" & A Coy up to 150 men failed also for the same reason as the first. Bn was withdrawn at 5 a.m. and marched back to KRUISSTRAAT. Casualties for night of 20th 21st 3 officers wounded & 61 other ranks 6 men killed and 40 missing.	
21st Feb	Spent the day in billets at KRUISSTRAAT and in the evening moved at 9 pm to the Infantry Barracks at YPRES. Casualties for second period in trenches Five officers wounded Lt. Colonel Enderby Capt & Adjt R. Field Lt. W. H. C. Bramston Lt. G. T. Legard 2nd Lt. W. Jenkins) 28 other ranks killed 105 wounded 43 missing.	
22nd	Spent the day in the Infantry Barracks	

16

Town, date and place	Summary of events and information	Remarks and references to Appendices
	at YPRES, in the evening received orders to move back next morning to BAILEUL. Men were given new boots which were urgently required.	
23rd Feb	Marched at 6.30 a.m. [via VLAMERTINGHE and WESTOUTRE] to BAILEUL which we reached about 11.30 a.m. [and were placed in billets in a side street off main square.]	FIFTH DIV^N
24th Feb	Bⁿ spent day in billets at BAILEUL. [two Coys went to baths in the evening and got change of underclothing.]	
25th Feb	In same billets as previous day. [remainder of Bⁿ went to baths. Coy Commanders went out in evening to see new trenches which Bⁿ are to occupy and returned next morning. Day spent in cleaning up, reclothing, and in instructing b.Cob and men of Grenadier Platoons in use of Bombs.]	

17

Hour, date and Place	Summary of events and Information	Remarks and references to appendices
26th Feb	Bn in Billets at BAILEUL in houses and barns. In the afternoon practice in Bomb throwing was given to men of Grenadier Platoons.	
27th Feb	Bn marched off at 4 p.m. for the trenches marching to WULVERGHEM via NEUVE EGLISE where men had teas. Trenches were taken over from Norfolk Regt, C & D Coys were in firing line and A & B in support in Farm Buildings. Quiet night, no casualties.	2/5
28th Feb	Quiet day, hardly any firing, in the evening "A"&"B" Coys relieved C.D [after having a hot meal at TEA FARM to which cook waggons and water carts were brought at nightly. 4th M.G. received from Ordnance and damaged gun returned to our BILLETS at DRANOUTRE for cleaning etc] No casualties	
1st March	Two Coys in trenches, two in Farm buildings in support. Trenches shelled twice during morning and sand bags knocked	

WAR DIARY

2nd NORTHUMBERLAND FUSILIERS

March

1915

1st March. — Two Coys in trenches, two in farm buildings in support. Trenches shelled thrice during morning & sandbags knocked

R parapet [but] no damage done. Casualties [occurred.] Draft of 109 N.C.O's and men arrived from ROUEN. draft composed largely of wounded men and men unfit when Bn left England. Heavy gun fire heard all night on our left flank but a long way off. Casualties one killed and one wounded

2nd March [Bn in trenches] Coys in fire trenches relieved under Bn arrangements at dark. Quiet day, no German shell fire. [Trenches visited at night by Territorial Officers and Cadets.] Heavy rifle fire from both sides on our right about 2.30 a.m following on our artillery fire. Casualties two men wounded during relief [by rifle fire]

3rd March [Bn in trenches] A & B Coys in fire trenches C & D in support. Fire trenches and Farm Building where supports

Hour, date and place	Summary of events and information	Remarks and reference to appendices
	where were shelled about 2.30 p.m, wire entanglements of 15a trench blown down but there were no casualties. Bn was relieved at 9 p.m by Welsh Regt except D Coy who remained in support at PACK HORSE FM and were under orders of O.C Welsh Regt. Remainder of Bn moved back to DRANOUTRE where they were billeted in Barns arriving there about 11 p.m	2/5
4th March	Bn in reserve in Billets at DRANOUTRE, D Coy still with Welsh Regt. men had baths at the Brewery	CASUALTIES for 3rd period in Trenches 1 killed 4 wounded.
5th March	Bn disposed as on previous day. men had baths at Brewery. Bn found a working party of 2 Officers and 100 men to dig new line of fire trench under R.E Officer, this party left at 4.30 p.m for NEUVE EGLISE	(N)2/Lt Ellis wounded

Hour, date and place	Summary of events and information	Remarks and references to appendices
	and got back about 2.45 a.m this day about 200x of fire trench and were complimented on their work. One man wounded [during the time working party were out] 2nd Lt Walker and 14 men from hospital joined on this date]	2/5
6th March	Bn still in billets in reserve [men had use of baths during day] Experiments were carried out during the morning with a Drain Pipe trench mortar, bombs were fired successfully but the exact angle required to hit the mark was not obtained, some of the shells fitted very badly into the mortar. 2nd Lt Sweet joined on first appointment]	
7th March	Bn disposed as on previous day [Chaplain held Church Service in a Barn for men of the Bn] Bn with transport less "D" Coy marched to BAILLEUL via KOUDEKOT and	

21

Hour, date and place	Summary of events and information	Remarks and reference to appendices
	took over same billets as we occupied before in the RUE DES MOULINS. D" Coy rejoined Bn at 9.45 p.m. from duty with Welsh Regt.	1/5

[Stamp: ORDERLY ROOM MAR 8 1915 2ND BN NORTHLD FUSILIERS]

Ghulzabor Smith
Comdg 2/Northd Fusiliers.
Major

Hour, date and place	Summary of events and information	Remarks and references to appendices
8th March	Battalion in Billets at BAILLEUL in the RUE DES MOULINS. Companies paraded for Drill and Rifle exercises.	
9th March	Battalion in Billets. Experiments with trench mortars carried out in the morning. N.C.O's and men practiced in the use of hand grenades.	
10th March	Battalion in same Billets. G.O.C. 84th Brigade made an inspection of the Battalion in Marching Order in the street outside Billets.	
11th March	Battalion in same Billets. Baths were allotted to us and two Coys were able to bathe and change clothing. Battalion marched out at 11pm to WULVERGHEM via DRANOUTRE and after drawing tools and ladders etc at R.E FARM were moved in to trenches as follows. "D" Coy in to 15 trench and 16 trench, remainder in dug outs in rear of 15 and	

Hour, date and place	Summary of events and information	Remarks and references to appendices
	14 B trench and in new trenches constructed during night. Battalion was ordered to attack German trenches in front of 16 and 15 trenches as soon as the attack by 7th Brigade on hill 75 succeeded.	76
12th March	Attack by 3rd Division timed for 8.40 a.m did not then take place owing to the fog. During morning Batteries fired to register and range and to destroy German wire entanglements. At 3 pm guns opened heavy fire on German trenches and after first half hour shells began to drop short and fell into 15 trench and into 16 trench wounding a number of men. Coys in support were also shelled by German guns. 4.10 pm attack by 7th Brigade commenced but did not succeed so no orders were	

Hour date and place	Summary of events and Information	Remarks and references to appendices
	given for 05th to attack. At 10 p.m. Battalion received orders to return to Billets at BAILLEUL which was reached about 3 a.m. Casualties 2nd Lt Cooper wounded and twenty four other ranks and five other ranks killed. Note about half of our wounded were due to our own shells bursting short.	
13th March	05th arrived back in Billets about 3 a.m and spent the day there.	
14th March	05th in Billets at BAILLEUL. Coys paraded for drill and practice in Grenade throwing.	
15th March	Same billets as previous day. Coys paraded for drill in morning.	
16th March	Bn in same billets as on previous day. Coys at drill parades in morning.	

25

Hour date and place	Summary of events and Information	Remarks and references to appendices
March 17th	[In same billets at BAILLEUL] in the afternoon [moved out and] took over new billets about 1½ miles out situated between ST JANS CAPPEL and METEREN ROADS. [Billets very scattered and very dirty.]	
March 18th	In billets at ST JANS CAPPEL [Coys paraded for drill in the morning. Billets and lines were thoroughly cleaned up.]	
March 19th	Moved off at 3.30 p.m for the trenches marched via ASYLUM and DRANOUTRE and halted for tea at LINDENHOEK. Took over trenches from Worcesters and from 4th Bn Rifle Brig. Our trenches from E1 to F2 inclusive. Bn H.Q at the CHALET LINDENHOEK, A & B Coys in trenches C & D in support	

Hour date and place	Summary of events and Information	Remarks and references to appendices
	at PONDFARM and in farm buildings at LINDENHOEK. Quiet during night	
20th March	Quiet day [a few shells passed over H.Q about 3 pm and burst on hill behind.] At night C & D Coys relieved A & B in trenches, 15 trench was taken over from 83rd Bde. [Brigade Major visited trenches.]	
21st March	Quiet day. German aeroplane came over LINDENHOEK and was fired at by antiaircraft guns, two German observation balloons seen in direction of MESSINES. A & B Coys relieved C & D in trenches F2 trench taken over by CHESHIRE Regt. About 9 pm rapid fire lasting for about 2 minutes was opened by Germans opposite	

Hour, date and place	Summary of events and Information	Remarks and reference to appendices
	15 trench.	
22nd March	Quiet day in trenches. C&D Coys relieved A&B in trenches at night. New support trenches commenced near FRENCHMAN'S FARM, also a dug out for H.Q. Working party of 1st Monmouths sent out to assist in making communication trenches.	
23rd March	A&B Coys to trenches in the evening in relief of C&D Coys. Quiet during day. [A Report came in at 1 a.m. that Germans were massing opposite F2, report proved incorrect and origin could not be traced.]	
24th March	Quiet day in trenches, at night Coys were relieved by Welch Regt. about 8.30 p.m. and marched [via DRANOUTRE] to the HUTS near LOCRE Village which were reached	

Hour date and place	Summary of events and Information	Remarks and reference to appendices
25th March	About 11.30 pm. Coys in huts near LOCRE transport at farm near KOUDEKOT. Coys had baths in DRANOUTRE in morning and afternoon.	Support Coys had to work hard each night digging communication trenches and new support trenches and got little rest. Casualties for period in trenches 2nd Lt G. R. L. Wyndham killed and four other ranks, wounded 15 other ranks
26th March	Coys in huts near LOCRE baths at DRANOUTRE again at our disposal. Working party of 500 men with 10 officers and NCO's went out at 6pm to FRENCHMANS FARM where they dug a communication trench 500 x long and 3'6" deep and 5' tread as far as the redoubt. Party got back about 3 am	
27th March	In huts near Locre baths in DRANOUTRE at our disposal. 2 officers and 4 NCO's sent to learn how to use a trench mortar.	

Hour, date and place	Summary of events and Information	Remarks and references to appendices
28th March	Brigade Church parade in field near DRANOUTRE. 5.30 pm marched off from LOCRE for trenches which were taken over from 1st Welch Regt. C & D Coys were in fire trenches with A & B Coys in support in farm buildings. Three trench mortars were used at night which fired 21 shells and put eleven of these into German trenches and silenced their mortars which had been very active on previous night.	
29th March	Quiet day. A & B Coys relieved C & D in fire trenches at night. 4 casualties during relief, a very bright moonlight night. No bombing done by either side.	
30th March	Quiet day. At night C & D Coys relieved A & B in fire trenches. Working parties from Welch Regt and Suffolk Regt came out	

Hour, date and place	Summary of events and Information	Remarks and references to appendices
31st March	from Pelleto and completed new communication trenches. German antiaircraft guns very active during morning. German artillery shelled WULVERGHEM in the afternoon. At night A & B Coys relieved C & D in trenches. Support Coys each found a platoon for work on communication trenches. German working party in front of 15 trench fired on with M. Gun.	

28th Division.
84th Infantry Brigade

WAR DIARY

2nd NORTHUMBERLAND FUSILIERS

April

1915

1st April	German guns active all day, especially anti-aircraft guns. About 3.30 pm Germans shelled our trenches and supporting point but did little damage beyond damaging a small part of the parapet. Bn. was relieved at night by Welch Regt and marched back to Billets at Locre which were reached about 11.30 pm. Casualties for tour of
	duty in the trenches. Three men died of wounds and fourteen wounded

Grahzel-a Peat
Comdg. 2/North'd Fusiliers
Major.

Hour, date and place	Summary of events and information	Remarks and references to appendices
2nd April	Battalion in huts at LOCRE. Baths in DRANOUTRE at our disposal during the day.	
3rd April	Marched at 10 a.m to Billets in farm houses near St Jans Cappel. Billets were very scattered and were situated between the BAILLEUL — ST JANS CAPEL and BAILLEUL — METEREN roads. These were the same billets as those occupied on the previous occasion when 85th came to ST JANS CAPEL.	
4th April	In billets in farm houses as on previous day. Church parade was held in the afternoon in the transport lines. Capt. Auld rejoined	
5th April	In billets as previous day	
6th April	In billets as previous day	
7th April	Genl Sir Horace Smith Dorrien inspected the 84th Bde at LOCRE and thanked us for past work done and	

33

Hour, date and place.	Summary of events and information	Remarks and references to appendices.
7th April	expressed himself pleased at the smart turnout of the Brigade; after the inspection we returned to billets.	
8th April	Brigadier Genl Bols commanding 84th Bde saw all the officers of the Battn and all men who had arrived during the past month	
9th April	Remained in billets company training	
10th April	Remained in billets company training	
11th April	The Bn was inspected by Lt General Sir Herbert Plumer who expressed his appreciation of their turn out and good work done in the past three months, and his pleasure at again having the Bn under his command	

Hour, date and place.	Summary of events and Information	Remarks and references to appendices
April 12th	The Bn remained in billets	
April 13th	The Bn paraded at 8.40am and marched via BAILLEUL Lunatic Asylum OUDERDOM and VLAMERTINGE to the New Huts camp situated between VLAMERTINGHE and YPRES where they went into camp. M-Genl Bulfin cmdg 28th Division paid an informal visit to the camp in the course of the afternoon. (The 84th Bde this day returned to 28th Division from which it had been temporarily detached since the 22nd of Feby)	

35

Hour, date and place.	Summary of events and Information	Remarks and references to appendices
April 14th	The B?? remained in billet the New Huts Camp training under company commanders.	
April 15th	The B?? Paraded at 5.45pm for duty in the trenches and relieved the 3rd 13th Royal Fusiliers in the trenches about 400 yds east of ZONNEBEKE. All four companies were in the fire trenches as it was thought that the Germans would attack during the night. The night however passed comparatively quietly	
April 16th	The Germans brought a minnen werfer to bear on the trenches occupied by 'C' and 'D' Coys reinforced by 3	

Hour, date and place	Summary of events and information	Remarks and references to appendices
	platoons of B Coy. This minnenwerfer fired over 100 shells and demolished about 150 yards of parapet on either side of the BROODSEINDE Cross Roads. Our Howitzers endeavoured to silence this minnenwerfer but without success. About 90 yards of the Parapet was re-built during the night. B Coy moved back into support	
April 17th	About 6.30 a.m. it was discovered that some Germans (probably about 20 to 30) had established themselves in the gap between C and D Coy trenches. C Coy was at once	

Hour, date and place.	Summary of events and information	Remarks and references to appendices
	re-inforced by one platoon of B Coy and it was decided to attack and drive back this party of Germans. Our Artillery fired so as to prevent the Enemy from bringing up his supports and A, C, and D Coys then attacked the enemy who were supported by fire from their own fire trenches. Hand grenades were largely used on both sides, in fact it is estimated that our companies threw over 300 and the enemy an equal number. By 7.30 AM all the enemy who had occupied the gap had been	

Hour, date and place.	Summary of events and information	Remarks and reference to appendices
	killed or wounded or driven back to their trenches. A number of grenades, two rifles and some equipment were captured by us. The Brigadier telephoned his congratulations and particularly congratulated Captain D. B. Foster on his initiative and energy. The remainder of the day was comparatively quiet until 5.30 pm when two German minnenwerfers again opened fire on the same sector of our trenches and broke down the parapet. One of these minnenwerfers was put out of action	

38

Hour, date & Place	Summary of events and information	Remarks and references to appendices
	by our artillery but the other continued to fire till we were relieved about 11 PM by the 1st Welch Regt. The Bn then returned to the New Huts camp just west of YPRES. Casualties during the tour of duty Wounded: 2° Lt B.S.S. Mahon 2° Lt A.H. Tuke Lt C.H. Markham Slightly wounded Capt A.C Hart Other ranks 14 killed 30 wounded nil missing	

Hour, date & Place	Summary of events and information	Remarks and references to appendices
18th	Remained in billets.	
19th	Training under Coy officers.	
20th	Training under Coy officers. The Battalion was placed at the disposal of the 5th Division and ordered to stand by to support if necessary the attack on hill 60. Later the Grenadiers under Lt. Walton (who was shortly afterwards wounded) were sent to reinforce the Cameron Highlanders with whom they remained for two days earning praise from the Brigadier of the 15th Bde.	

Hour, date & Place	Summary of events and information	Remarks and references to appendices
21st April	The Bn was ordered to march to ZILLEBEKE Pond to be at the disposal of the 15th Bde Commander. The Bn occupied dugouts in the bank and remained in Local Reserve till the evening of the 23rd being continually subjected to Hostile Shrapnel Fire	
22nd April	The Battalion received orders to return to its hutments and to stand by at the disposal of G.O.C. 28th Division	
23rd April	The Battalion relieved (St. George's Day) the 1st Battalion of the Welch Regt. in the trenches just south of ZONNEBEKE. YPRES was heavily	

Hour, date and place	Summary of events and information	Remarks and references to appendices
	shelled as we passed through and Captain E. H. Baxter was wounded. 1 man killed and 5 others wounded.	
24th April	'C' Coy. and 2 platoons of A Coy. plus 2 companies of the Cheshire Regt. were sent under Major Moulton-Barrett to support the Canadians S.W. of the ZONNEBEKE—St JULIEN ROAD. 'C' Coy. and the 2 platoons of A Coy. reinforced the Canadian trenches while the two companies of Cheshire Regt. remained in support. Two German attacks were repulsed.	
25th April	The Germans fired shell containing poisonous gas which made the eyes smart and water. Some 30 Germans broke through	

Hour, date and place	Summary of events and information	Remarks and references to Appendices
	between our left and the E. Surrey Regt., right at ZONNEBEKE but 18 were captured and the remainder killed. Continuous hostile shell fire on fire trenches and supports all day. The Germans made 4 seperate attacks on our trenches but were repulsed. Major Moulton-Barrett's mixed detachment covered the retirement of the 6th D.L.I. (who had evacuated their trenches) and took up a position just south of the ZONNEBEKE-St JULIEN ROAD to prevent the Germans advancing through the gap thus made in the line.	

Hour, date and Place	Summary of events and Information	Remarks and references to appendices
26th April	A quiet day in the trenches at ZONNEBEKE but a strenuous day for Major Moulton-Barrett's mixed detachment who were storming the advance of a greatly superior force of the enemy. Major E.M. Barrett was wounded early in the morning and Capt. & Adjt. R Auld sent out to take over the command of the mixed detachment. The mixed detachment nearly got surrounded and cut off but Captain Auld sent back an urgent appeal for reinforcements which arriving in time enabled him to hold on for the rest of the day. The Germans ever attempting to press home their attack. At midnight after removing the	

Hour date and Place	Summary of events and Information	Remarks and references to appendices
	removing the wounded the mixed detachment now re-inforced by 6 machine guns and a Coy. of the Welch Regt took up a more favourable position and entrenched where it remained till the evening of the 28th being subjected to continuous heavy shell fire but never being properly attacked. Other Battalions were hurried up during these two days and the gap was effectually closed	
27th April	The Minnenwerfer destroyed a considerable amount of our parapet in both 31 + 32 trenches.	
28th April	The mixed detachment now commanded by Capt. Auld was relieved	

Hour date and Place	Summary of events and information	Remarks and references to Appendices
	and C Coy and the platoon of A Coy rejoined the Battalion. An uneventful day in the ZONNEBEKE trenches.	
April 29th	The Battn remained in trenches	2/5 A
April 30th	The Battn remained in trenches	

28th Division.
54th Inf. Bde.
84th

WAR DIARY

2nd NORTHUMBERLAND FUSILIERS

               31st
1st to 4th MAY 1915

47

Hour, date and place	Summary of events and Information	Remarks and references to appendices
	and A and C Companies evacuated at 10.30 pm leaving each a party of 30 NCOs and men under Lieuts Dugard and Tuke. These remained till midnight evacuating two complete companies and then withdrew to join the Batt'n.	
May 4th	The Batt'n reached the Hutments just North of the Ypres & Vlamertinghe road early in the morning and went into Reserve. Casualties during the tour of duty from April 21st to May 4th 6 Officers wounded O.R. 35 Killed 149 Wounded 17 Missing	R W Mahon Lt Col Lieut Col Comdg 3/North'n Fusiliers

Hour, date and place	Summary of events and information	Remarks and references to appendices
May 4th	Battalion ordered out at p.m. to support of Cheshire Regt at POTIJIE. Remained in G.H.Q line in Support.	
5th	Battalion still in support at POTIJIE.	
6th	Battalion relieved the 1st Bn Welch Regt in the trenches about midnight. These trenches were situated to the north of the village WIELTJE, BELGIUM, about ¾ of a mile, with the left of the Battn astride the St JULIEN road and the right resting on the FORTUIN road.	
7th	The enemy made an attack on the trenches held by the Battn which was repulsed. Our guns then took up the fire & shelled the enemy. 2/Lieut. A.S. Luke killed Sergts Taylor & Shaxman killed	

Hour, date and place.	Summary of events and Information	Remarks and references to appendices
	The Germans continued shelling the position all day.	Capt. Stephen 2/Lt. M.V. O'Dowd Joined
8th.	At about 3.30 the enemy's guns opened fire with high explosive & shrapnel which increased in volume about 7am and continued all day till the enemy's infantry delivered their attack upon the right of the line held by the 84th Inf Bde. at about 3.30 p.m. The line of trenches extended from the road St JULIEN to the ZONNEBEKE Road ~~West~~ NORTH of VERLOREN HOEK. which were held by the following units commencing on the right 2nd Bn Cheshire Regt 1st Bn Suffolk Regt 1st Monmouthshire Regt 3rd Bn Royal Fus. The line at the Cheshires was broken and the enemy got through to	

Hour, date and place	Summary of events and Information	Remarks and references to appendices
May 8th	the rear & enveloped the Suffolk Regt. The Monmouths fell back & made a counter attack which failed, and from information obtained the enemy outflanked & held the D.C. & B Coy. No. 1, 2 & 3 platoons (A Coy) under [illegible] held on to their trenches and fought gallantly. Their devotion to duty saved the situation. These platoons were relieved at 4 am on the 9th by detachments of the East Lancs Regt. The following casualties occurred Lieut Colonel S.A. Enderby. Capt Rauld Lieut A.B. Cramsie M.G. Off. Lieut J.K. Manger Scout Off. A Coy Capt. A.C. Hart Killed	P of W ~~Missing~~ P of W do Killed Wounded + Missing

Hour, date and place	Summary of events and Information	Remarks and references to appendices
8th.	2/Lieut R. Lord wounded	
	2/Lieut W. Watson wounded.	
	B Company	
	Capt G.K Molineux	missing
	2/Lieut W Taylor wounded	P of W
	C Company	
	Lieut B.E.S. Mahon	P of W
	2/Lieut B.C. Hardy	P of W
	D Company	
	Lieut G.P. Legard Killed	
	2/Lieut K Shann Killed	
	2/Lieut R.S. Taylor wounded	
	attached	
	2/Lieut E.B.A. Cardew	P of W
	4th Devon Regt	missing
	NCO + men, killed wounded + missing 422 (x)	(x) Killed 12, Wounded 126, missing 284 } 422
9th.	The following rejoined	
	Transport Headquarters	
	2/Lt G.H. Steel	
	2/Lt. W.H.C. Bucknall.	
	A. Coy 65. B Coy 25	
	C Coy 18. D Coy 8 Total 116	
	The following draft	
	arrived from 3rd Bn.	
	2/Lieuts C.R Freeman, H.C Hobbs	
	W.G.B Garrard + 248 men	

Hour, date and place	Summary of events and information	Remarks and references to appendices
9th	Batn reformed. Capt H C Stephen assumed command, & Capt & Qr m W.M. Allan assumed duties of Adjt + Transport Officer. Strength 10 officers + 457 n.c.o.men. Capt H C Stephen Capt & Qr m W.M. Allan 2/Lieut C R Freeman " W H C Bucknall " W G B Garrard " H E Hobbs " M V O'Dowd " R V Taylor " A C Steel Lieut J M Gillespie RAMC Batn in billets near POPERINGHE	
10	Batn moved to B Huts near Ypres in support	
11th	Batn formed with detail 1/Suffolk & 2nd Cheshire Regt into a composite battalion under Major Toke 1/ Welch Regt and	

Hour, date and place	Summary of events and information	Remarks and references to appendices
11th	moved to farm 26 Rue d'ELVERDINGHE	
12th	moved to billets at [LYSSENT HOECK], POPERINGHE	
13th	In billets at above place	
14	5 a.m. moved to Bivouac in Balloon Wood North of POPERINGHE + VLAMERTINGHE road.	
15	Battn still in bivouac Stood to ARMS 4 A.M. to 8 A.M.	
16th	Battn still at Balloon Wood. Stood to Arms 8pm to 12 m.n.	
17th	Battn still at Balloon Wood. Stood to Arms 8pm to 12 m.n. Capt R M L & Booth + 2/Lt J.H. Sellers joined	
18th	Battalion remained in Bivouac at Balloon Wood	
19th	Battalion marches at 11am to Herzeele Billeted on Dutters Farm	

Hour, date and place.	Summary of events and Information	Remarks and references to appendices
May 25th – 31st	Battalion resting. 84th Infy Bde paraded on the Square at Herzeele, and was inspected by the Field Marshal Comdg in Chief at Noon. The following is a precis of his speech :— "I came over to say a few words to you & to tell you how much I, as Comdr in Chief of this army, appreciate the splendid work that you have all done during the recent fighting. You have fought the second battle of YPRES which will rank among the most desperate & hardest fights of the war. You may have thought because you were no attacking the enemy that you were not helping to shorten the	

55

Hour, date and place	Summary of events and Information	Remarks and references to appendices
21st	the war. On the contrary by your splendid endurance & bravery, you have done a great deal to shorten it. In this, the second battle of Ypres, the Germans tried by every means in their power to get possession of that unfortunate town. They concentrated large forces of troops & Arty, and further than that they had recourse to that mean & dastardly practice hitherto unheard of in civilised warfare, namely the use of asphyxiating gases. You have performed the most difficult, arduous & terrific task of withstanding a stupendous bombardment by heavy Arty, probably the fiercest artillery	

Hour, date and place.	Summary of events and information	Remarks and references to appendices
	fire ever directed against troops, and warded off the enemy's attack with magnificent bravery. By your steadiness & devotion, both the German plans were frustrated. He was unable to get possession of YPRES — if he had done this he would probably have succeeded in preventing neutral powers from intervening — and he was also unable to distract us from delivering our attack in conjunction with the French in ARRAS-ARMENTIERES district. Had you failed to repulse his attack, and made it necessary for more troops to be sent to your assistance, our oper-	

...ur, date and place	Summary of events and Information	Remarks and references to appendices
	ations in the South might not have been able to take place and would certainly not have been as successful as they have been. Your Colours have many famous names emblazoned on them but none will be more famous or more well deserved than that Second Battle of YPRES. I want you one & all to understand how thoroughly I realise & appreciate what you have done. I wish to thank you, each officer, non-commissioned officer and man for the services you have rendered by doing your duty so magnificently,	

Hour, date and place	Summary of events and information	Remarks and references to appendices
	and I am sure that your country will thank you too." 151 men joined the Battalion.	
22	Battalion [now reformed] marched to Farm nr Poperinghe on Elverdinghe road	
23	Remained in billets.	
24	Battalion ordered out in support. marched at 6 am [halted at railway crossing 1 mile west of YPRES. till noon. when it marched via KRUISSTRAAT. to railway crossing west of YPRES. thence skirting North of railway to ~~road~~ ~~and~~ ~~enemy~~	

58

Hour, date and place	Summary of events and Information	Remarks and references to appendices
	a point where the railway crosses the MENIN road. The Battn was formed in 3 lines for the attack of WITEPOORT FARM. & the ridge on which it stood. A Coy led C Company following, D Company in the 3rd line. B Coy in support. The attack on the farm & ridge was successful, & the companies dug themselves in behind the hedge west of the road running in front of the farm. The 2nd attack was developed from this point directed on BELLEWAARDE Farm, during this attack the bomb.Offr, Capt C.S. Wreford Brown, was killed. Lieut E.H. Salis. assumed command & led the 2nd attack during which he was	

Hour, date and place	Summary of events and information	Remarks and references to appendices
24th	wounded. The position on the ridge was strengthened & held. Casualties:-	
	1 Capt. C Wreford Brown DSO	Killed
	2 " R M Ely Booth, DSO	Wounded
	" H C Stephen	Wounded
	8 Lieut. C H Salic	Wounded
	" D A de C Buckle	Wounded
	" J H Hogshaw	Wounded
	" C R Freeman	Wounded
	" W H C Bucknall	Wounded
	" A E Hobbs	Wounded
	" W G B Garrard	Wounded
	1 " J A Sellers	Killed
	" M V O'Dowd	Wounded
	Lieut J M Gillespie RAMC	missing
	Men Killed 29	
	Wounded 133	
	Missing 188.	
25th	Remainder of Battalion continued in action	
26th	Battalion in billets NORTH of Road 2 miles from POPERINGHE – YPRES	

Hour, date and place	Summary of events and Information	Remarks and references to appendices
27th	In Billets as on 26th	
28th	10 men joined Batt'n. Battalion marched to Herzeele to rest & refit. Billeted on Schipmans Farm	
29th	Capt. W.T. Rushbrook Lieut. A.R. Barkworth 2/Lt. R.B. Sowell — 1/5 Bn. Nor. Stafford " G. Clarke — 3rd Bn. Nor. Stafford & 40 men joined Batt'n. Batt'n inspected by Lieut Gen'l Allenby V th Corps Commander. in the Public Square with remainder of Brigade.	& assumes Command.
30th 31st	Resting — 2/Lieut G. Wilkins joined. The Batt'n was visited by Mr Ben Tillett M.P. who addressed the men & thanked them for the brave & gallant work they had done in the field for the maintenance of the liberty & freedom enjoyed by every Britisher.	

Tom Felan Capt fr
Commanding 7/north Fus.

84th Bde.
28th Division.

2nd NORTHUMBERLAND FUSILIERS:

JUNE

1915

Date and place	Summary of events and information	Remarks and references to appendices
June 1st	Resting	
June 2nd	Route march in morning. Resting. Baths for men	
June 3rd	Bn attended Brigade Parade to celebrate Birthday of H.M. The King.	
June 4th	Bn resting. Route march.	
June 5th	Bn resting, draft of 220 NCO's & men arrived including 30 men who had been out before and 96 men transferred from 3rd D.L.I.	
June 6th	Bn attended divine Service in HERZEELE.	
June 7th	Route march. Maj General BULFIN cmdg 28th Division visited the Bn.	
June 8th	Bn still at HERZEELE The following officers joined. Lieut: Hopkinson A.J. Lieut Kingdon F.C. 2Lt Allgood A.J. 2Lt Bacon D.F.C. 2Lt Wright C.C.J.	4th Bn Durham Light Infantry 3rd Bn North'd Fus. 4th Bn Durham Light Infantry "

Hour date and place	Summary of events and information	Remarks and references to Appendices
June 9th	Bn still resting in billets at HERZEELE	
June 10th	Bn still resting. Brigade route march. Practice throwing bombs. Three men accidentally wounded.	Major C.A. Armstrong joined the battalion at noon and took over the command.
June 11th	Battalion left HERZEELE and marched to RENNINGHELST arriving about 8 p.m. Went into huts at ROZENHILL BECK for the night	
June 12th	Battalion left ROZENHILL BECK and marched to the trenches at 7.30 p.m. arriving about 12 midnight. Batt relieved 7th Rifle Brigade. B and C Coys in firing line – B Coy in redoubt, A Coy in support – D Coy in reserve – one casualty in C Coy – (killed)	

Hour, date and Place	Summary of events and Information	Remarks and references to Appendices
13th June	Situation quiet all day. Weather fine — Casualty one (wounded) C Coy.	
14th June	Situation quiet — Weather fine. Germans reported to be sapping under P3 trench (Suffolk Regt). Lt. A.R. BARKWORTH other ranks three (wounded)	WOUNDED. 2 of C Coy. 1 of B Coy.
15th June	Situation unchanged — In the morning G.O.C 28th Divn visited Battn Hd Qrs. Casualties one (wounded) C Coy.	
16th June	Weather fine — Situation quiet. Royal Engineers blew up sapping done by Germans under P3 trench, about 3 o'clock in the morning. Casualties five (wounded)	2 B Coy. 1 D Coy. 1 C Coy. 1 A Coy.

Hour, date and Place	Summary of events and Information	Remarks and references to Appendices
17th June	Weather fine – Battn Hd Qrs shelled about 5 p.m. Ten shells dropped – five hitting the BRASSERIE – Medical officer was the only casualty – Lt J. COWAN RAMC other ranks one (wounded)	Wounded. C Coy.
18th June	Situation quiet – Weather fine. Lt W BAXTER RAMC joined Battn about 2 A.M. Capt R.M.K LAMB joined Battn about 9 p.m and took over duty as Second in Command. Casualties five (wounded) O2 trench relieved by the WELSH Regiment.	4 C Coy. 1 A Coy.
19th June	Situation quiet all day – Weather fine – Casualties – Nil –	
20th June	Situation quiet – Weather fine. Lt B.D CREW and 2Lt C W POLLOCK 3rd DURHAM LIGHT INFANTRY joined the Battn; Lt W BAXTER RAMC relieved by Lt H B TAYLOR RAMC	"

Hour, date, place	Summary of events and information	Remarks and references to Appendices
20th June (cont)	Casualties one (wounded)	A Coy.
21st June	Situation quiet and unchanged. 2nd Lt. J. WALTON, 2 Lt JOHNSTON 2nd Lt BAKER joined the Batt. C Coy. relieved by D Coy.	
22nd June	Weather fine – Very heavy bombardment for over an hour – North of our front in the direction of HOOGE. Casualties one (wounded)	C Coy.
23rd June	Situation quiet – weather fine. Batt. relieved about 11 pm by 3rd Batt. Royal Fusiliers. Relief was completed successfully and Batt. marched back to PIONEER FARM, arriving there about 2.15 A.M. Casualties 5 (wounded)	3 back at duty.
24th June	Batt. at PIONEER FARM. B and C Coys. went into the trenches and relieved YORK and LANCASTER regiment. Relief carried out successfully	B Coy & 2 platoons of C Coy in fire trenches. Other 2 platoons of C Coy in defences at VIERSTRAAT

...ar, date and place	Summary of events and information	Remarks and references to appendices
24th June (cont)	Casualties - nil. A and D Coys: still at PIONEER FARM	
25th June	B and C Companys in trenches at WERSTRAAT. A and D Companys at PIONEER FARM. Heavy rain in the afternoon. 2nd Lt C.B. Corlson and 2nd Lt O. Carr-Ellison joined the Battn with 29 men returned from hospital. Casualties nil.	
26th June	Half Battn still in trenches other half at PIONEER FARM. 2nd Lt. Craig 2nd Lt. Walkmonyt 2nd Lt. Hamilton 2nd Lt. Bramwell } Joined the Battn 26th June Joined the Battn about 8 p.m. Casualties nil.	Appendix ... ... July the appendix ... ... at WERSTRAAT.

Hour, date and place	Summary of events and information	Remarks and references to appendices
27th June.	2 Coys: still in trenches remainder in support at PIONEER FARM, South of DICKEBUSCH. Casualties one	died of wounds.
28th June.	A and D relieved B and C Coys: respectively. Relief carried out successfully. Casualties one	A Coy: & 2 platoons of D Coy in fire trench. Other 2 platoons of D Coy in dugouts at VIERSTRAAT wounded.
29th June.	A and D Coys: in trenches B and C Coys: at PIONEER FARM. Casualties three	wounded.
30th June.	A and D Coys: in trenches B and C Coys: at PIONEER FARM. Enemy dropped high explosive shells on VIERSTRAAT in the morning and DICKEBUSCH in the afternoon. Working party of 100 men made a new support trench behind M1. Work carried out successfully. Casualties nil.	Cllumbert Major commanding 2nd Batt Scottish [?]

84th Bde.
28th Div.

2nd NORTHUMBERLAND FUSILIERS

J U L Y

1 9 1 5

Hour, date and place	Summary of events and Information	Remarks and references to appendices
1st July:	Battn still in trenches and at PIONEER FARM VIERSTRAAT slightly shelled in the afternoon, also M1 trench. Part of parapet of M1 listening post blown down. Casualties nil.	
2nd July:	B and C Coys: relieved A and D Coys: ½ B Coy: in defences at VIERSTRAAT, C Coy: and ½ B Coy: in M1 fire trench. Relief carried out successfully. Concert at 6 pm by 28th Divnl signal section. Casualties nil.	
3rd July:	B & C Coys: in trenches and at VIERSTRAAT. Situation quiet all day. Casualties nil.	

Hour, date and place.	Summary of events and Information	Remarks and references to appendices
July 4th	B and C Coys: in trenches and at VIERSTRAAT. A and D Coys: had the baths in DICKEBUSCH from 9.30 am – 12.30 pm and from 1.30 pm – 3.30 pm. Service for Wesleyans at 12.15 pm. C. of E. service at 5 pm. Brigade band attended. Casualties nil.	
July 5th	B and C Coys: still in trenches and at VIERSTRAAT. VIERSTRAAT shelled in the afternoon. No damage done. One horse set on fire. Casualties one	wounded.
July 6th	B and C Coys: still in trenches and at VIERSTRAAT. Working party on Subsidiary line. Lt. A.J. Hopkinson slightly wounded. No other Casualties	

Hour date and place.	Summary of events and information	Remarks and references to appendices
7th	B and C Coys. in trenches and at VIERSTRAAT. Situation quiet all day. 2nd Lt. Pollock wounded through the chest while with permanent digging party on Subsidiary line. No other casualties.	
8th	B and C Coys. relieved by A and D Coys. ½ A Coy. in defences at VIERSTRAAT, D Coy. and other ½ A Coy. in MI trench. Enemy made use of trench mortar killing some of our men. Our artillery replied effectively. Casualties 4 killed 1 wounded	Relief carried out successfully. Enemy made use of MINEWERFER
9th	A and D Coys. in trenches B and C Coys. at PIONEER FARM. Situation quiet. Casualties nil.	

72

Hour, date and place.	Summary of events and Information	Remarks and references to appendices
10th	A and D Coys: in trenches. B and C Coys: at PIONEER FARM. Enemy shelled DICKEBUSCH pretty heavily about 1 p.m. Two officers* and one man wounded through a bomb accident in C Coy: billet. 2nd Lt. J.C. WATMOUGH killed in the trenches about 2 p.m. One man seriously wounded in the trenches. B and C Coys: went to the baths in DICKEBUSCH in the morning. Casualties for the day. Officers 3 other ranks 2	*2nd Lt. Walton 2nd Lt. Craig
11th	A and D Coys: in trenches and at VIERSTRAAT. B & C Coys: at PIONEER FARM. Situation quiet. Wesleyan service 11.45 am Roman Catholic " 1 pm Church of England 5 pm with Brigade band. 2nd Lt. J.C. WATMOUGH was buried behind RIDGWOOD. D Coy: captured German prisoner. He was marched back to PIONEER FARM and then on to Hd Qrs 88th Bde	(Bavarian)

Hour, date and place	Summary of events and information	Remarks and references to appendices
11th (contd)	Casualties nil.	
12th	A and D Coys: relieved by Suffolk Regiment. Relief carried out successfully. A, D and C Coys: went into billets NORTH-EAST of KEMMEL HILL. B Coy: billeted at PIONEER FARM for the night. Casualties one	wounded.
13th	A, C & D Coys: in billets NORTH-EAST of KEMMEL. H.Q. & B Coy: at PIONEER FARM.	
14th	Coys: in same dispositions. Batt. stood by ready to move at half an hour's notice, from 9 pm till 9 AM 15th July. Lt. Taylor and 2 Lt. Fordham went out to reconnoitre KEMMEL SHELTERS. Lt. Hopkinson rejoined from hospital	

74

Hour, date and place.	Summary of events and information	Remarks and references to appendices
15th	Batt. moved to KEMMEL SHELTERS from billets NORTH-EAST of KEMMEL and PIONEER FARM. Move completed successfully. Three machine guns under Lt Taylor in supporting points 8:9:10 under command of O.C 1st Welsh regiment.	
16th	Batt. still in KEMMEL SHELTERS	
17th	Batt. still resting at KEMMEL SHELTERS.	
18th	Batt. still resting. Furnished a fatigue party of 150 men for work on VIA GELLIA and BATTLE Hd Qrs.	
19th	Batt. still at KEMMEL SHELTERS	

Hour, date and place.	Summary of events and information	Remarks and references to appendices
20th	Batt: marched out at 2.a.m for digging purposes near KEMMEL VILLAGE. Batt: digging dug outs for winter quarters.	
21st	A and C Coys: came back to KEMMEL SHELTERS. B and D Coys: remained in the wood digging. A draft of 159 men and one officer joined the Batt: about 9.p.m.	148 from 3rd W. YORKSHIRE REGT 11 rejoined men 2nd Lt. W.E Jenkins.
22nd	Coys: in same dispositions. We formed a carrying party of 80 men and 1 officer for mining section.	
23rd	B and D Coys: came back from digging and 1st 6th Welsh Regiment took over. B Coy + ½ D Coy: went into billets behind Regt H.Q Coy, A + C Coys: in KEMMEL SHELTERS	

Date and Place	Summary of events and information	Remarks and references to appendices
24th	A draft of 100 men from 3rd Battn. joined the Battn. Strength of Coys. now about 226 with transport. Coys. in same dispositions.	
25th	Coys. in same dispositions. Church parade 9.30 A.M.	
26th	Battn. disposed as for 25th. Coy Comdrs. reconnoitred trenches to be occupied night 27/28. Draft trained in Fire Discipline & care of arms.	
27th	Battn. took over line of trenches E of KEMMEL held by 1st Suffolk Regt. All Coys. holding firing line trenches with supports behind. C Coy 1 Platoon in Battn. reserve in KEMMEL Schools and	

77

Hour, date and place	Summary of event and Information	Remarks and references to appendices
27th Cont	25 men in Supporting Points. Relief completed without casualty.	
28th	Situation quiet & unchanged.	
29th	Situation quiet & unchanged. Casualty 1 man wounded. KEMMEL shelled by enemy during afternoon no damage done.	
30th	Situation quiet & unchanged. In late afternoon enemy put several shells over A Coy trench no damage done. Intense bombardment to the N took place about 3.15 a.m. till 5.30 p.m. A draft of 100 joined Bn at 7.30 p.m from 15th (Service) Batt. Casualties 1 men wounded	

Hour, date and place	Summary of events and information	Remarks and references to appendices
31st	Situation quiet & unchanged till about 1 a.m. 1 Aug when enemy caused 4 violent explosions on our parapet. The cause of the explosions was not ascertained. They might have been bombs but the explosions appeared too heavy. The Germans did not leave their trenches. The artillery was rung up & placed 2 shells in the German trenches. At 1.58 a.m. 1 Aug we blew in a German mine successfully under B Coy & undoubtedly caught the Germans at work on their mine. Casualties 2 Killed 2 wounded 2 Lieuts K D Woodroffe B C Woodroffe S A Rose and H J Holmes joined the Battⁿ for duty & were posted to Coys.	C H Armstrong Lt Col Comdg 2 North^d Fus

84th Bde.
28th Div.

2nd NORTHUMBERLAND FUSILIERS

A U G U S T

1 9 1 5

On His Majesty's Service.

Hour date and place	Summary of events and information	Remarks and references to appendices
1 Aug.	Situation quiet & unchanged. Casualties 1 killed and 1 wounded.	All casualties are up to 12 noon on date of entry.
Aug 2.	Battⁿ relieved by 1/6 Welch Reg & 1 Welsh Reg. Two machine guns remaining 1 in the fire trench & 1 in supporting point. Battⁿ marched back to billets at LOCRE. Casualties nil.	
Aug 3.	Battⁿ resting in tents & billets LOCRE.	
Aug 4.	Battⁿ resting at LOCRE. Coys at disposal of Coy Comdrs. 1 Officer & 2 NCOs per Coy attended a demonstration of bomb-throwing.	

Date and place	Summary of events and information	Remarks and references to appendices
Aug 5th	Resting at LOCRE. Coy drill. Communicating app drill. Training of spare Machine Gunners	
6th	Resting at LOCRE. Coy drill. Training of extra MG men, bomb-men & signallers. Draft of 27 OR joined 17 returned men	
7th	Resting at LOCRE. Coy drill. Training of extra MG men, bomb men & signallers.	
8th	Resting at LOCRE. Church parade 10 a.m.	
9th	Marched from LOCRE at 7.30pm to KEMMEL and took over trenches from 1st Welch Reg. ½ C Coy Batt. Reserve remainder occupying fire & support trenches &	

Hour date and place	Summary of events and information	Remarks and references & appendices
9th cont.	supporting points. Relief carried out without casualties. One Coy 7th (Serv) Bn Leicester Reg attached for instruction in trench duties.	
10th	Situation quiet & unchanged. Casualty 1 man wounded	
11th	Situation quiet & unchanged. Coy of 7th (Serv) Bn Leicester Reg attached for instruction relieved by another Coy of same Reg. ~~[struck through]~~ Casualties 1 man wounded also 1 man of Coy 7th Bn Leicester Reg wounded	
12th	Situation quiet & unchanged Casualty 1 man killed	

Hour, date and place.	Summary of events and Information	Remarks and references to appendices
13th	Situation quiet & unchanged. One Coy 7th Leicester Reg took over [illegible] as a Coy trenches held by their Batt. The Coy 7th Leicester Reg attached for instruction & which was divided up among [illegible] the Batt was withdrawn. Relief carried out successfully. [illegible] C.O.	Draft of 6 men trained as machine gunners joined
14th	Situation quiet & unchanged. The Coy 7th Leicester Reg returned to their Coy of their own Regt. We blew up a [illegible] a German mine which was working towards our trench held by B Coy. Casualty one was wounded.	
15th	Situation quiet & unchanged. Our fire trench taken over by 6 Welsh Reg. Casualties [illegible] were wounded.	

Hour, date place	Summary of events and information	Remarks and references to appendices
Aug 16	Situation quiet in the line. Casualties: 1 w.w. wounded	
Aug 17	Situation normal. Batt'n relieved in the trenches C & part D Coy by 23rd Inf Bde A B & part D Coy by 1st Welch Reg. Relief carried through without casualty. Enemy blew up a mine about 4.30 p.m. damaging a bay of the trench held by B Coy. Casualty: 1 o.r. wounded	One dug out destroyed in explosion, 1 man buried [?]
Aug 18	Resting KEMMEL shelter. Coy & Coy Officers disposed as usual. Casualties 3 wounded from mine explosion on 17th. Baths at LOCRE for men. Training spare time for [?] in [?]	

Hour, date and place	Summary of events and information	Remarks and reference to appendices
19 Aug	Resting KEMMEL shelters. Coys on instruction in handling of arms, extended order. Training attack & attack on movement. Bath. at LOCRE for men. 6 Officers 200 men Brigade fatigue at 8.15 p.m.	
20 Aug.	Resting KEMMEL shelters. Training as on 19th. Draft of 20 men joined	
21 Aug	Situation as on 20th. 6 Officers 610 OR employed on Brigade working party 8 p.m. to 10 a.m. 22nd.	
22 Aug.	Resting KEMMEL shelters. Church parade 10-30 a.m. 1 Officer 5 OR employed on Brigade working party. 8 p.m. – 10 a.m. 23rd. Casualty 1 Officer wounded	2nd Lieut C E HAMILTON.

Hour, date and place	Summary of events and Information	Remarks and references to appendices
23 Aug.	Resting KEMMEL Shelters. Coys at disposal of OC Coys training Bombers, Lewis Ma-chines, Snipers, in platoon.	
24 Aug	Batt relieved 1st W'md Reg A, C & D Coys in line + support trenches. B Coy (Coys) + Hars in supporting points, remainder of Coy Bn reserve. Casualties nil.	
25 Aug.	Situation quiet Casualties nil.	
26 Aug.	Situation quiet Casualties 2 men wounded. Draft of 10 men joined.	
27 Aug.	Situation quiet Casualty 1 man wounded.	
28 Aug	Situation quiet Casualty 1 man wounded.	

87

Hour, date and Place	Summary of events and Information	Remarks & references to appendices
29 Aug	Situation quiet during day. Casualties 3 men killed 1 man wounded.	
30 Aug	B⁺ relieved in the trenches by 1ˢᵗ Welch Reg. Marched back to KEMMEL Shelters. Casualties 2 men wounded	
31 Aug	Coy at disposal of O/C Coys marched at 3.30 pm to Badajos Huts & are relieving Cheshire Reg⁺ & handing over to them at Kemmel Shelters.	

Rh Lamb Capt & Lt Col
Com'dg 2/ North'd Fusiliers

84th Bde.
28th Div.

2nd NORTHUMBERLAND FUSILIERS

S E P T E M B E R

1 9 1 5

On His Majesty's Service.

88

Hour Date and Place	Summary of Events and Information	Remarks & references to appendices
1st Sept	At Locre Badajoz Huts. Coys at disposal of O/C Coys. Training Bombers & Sigs. Fatigue Uservice at Sans 150 men 3 officers.	
2nd Sept	At Locre Coys at Musketry Bayonet Fighting 40 men fatigue 235 men 8 Officers fatigue night 2/3rd	
3rd Sept	Batt moved from LOCRE to KEMMEL SHELTERS taking over from Suffolk Regt Fatigues A Coy 15 men night 3/4th 2 parties of 60 men fatigue.	
~~4 Sept~~	Divine Service at KEMMEL Shelters 10 am Batt reviewed 1st Welch Regt in trenches E of KEMMEL B C & D Coy 8 Coy party	Cancelled. Cap.

89

Hour, date and Place	Summary of events and information	Remarks & references to appendices
4 Sept	Batt⁰ at KEMMEL Shelters. Conf on fire discipline. Care of arms. Rapid firing. Training Bombers, Signallers & M.G. teams.	
5 Sept	Divine Service KEMMEL Shelters 10.15 a.m. Batt⁰ relieved 1st Welsh Reg. in trenches E. of KEMMEL. B.C & D Coys holding fire & support trenches. B Coy also garrisoning 2 supporting points. All M.G.s in fire trenches. A Coy Batt⁰ reserve KEMMEL schools. Bn. HQ at Doctors House.	
6 Sept	Situation quiet. Casualties 2 men wounded.	

Hour, Date and Place	Summary of events and information	Remarks and references to appendices
7 Sept.	Situation quiet & unchanged. Casualties 1 man died of wounds.	
8 Sept.	Situation quiet & unchanged.	
9 Sept.	Situation quiet & unchanged. Casualties 1 man died of wounds.	
10 Sept.	Situation quiet & unchanged.	
11 Sept.	Situation quiet. Batt⁰ relieved in the trenches by 1st Welch. Reg⁰ On relief Batt⁰ marched to billets KEMMEL shelters. Casualties 1 man killed.	
12 Sept.	Batt⁰ at KEMMEL shelters. Divine Service in a.m. At 2.30pm Batt⁰ marched to LOCRE & took over huts.	

91

Hour, date and Place	Summary of events and information	Remarks and references to appendices
3 Sept.	Battⁿ at LOCRE. Training Bombers, Signallers, Snipers, MG teams. Coys. Drill Handling arms. Musketry.	
4 Sept.	Battⁿ at LOCRE. Battⁿ inspected at 2.45 p.m. drawn up in mass by GOC 2nd Army.	
5 Sept.	Battⁿ marched to KEMMEL Shelters after dinner. 7 Officers 416 OR on R.E. working party 7pm to 12 M.N.	
6 Sept.	Battⁿ at KEMMEL shelters. Training Bombers, Snipers, Signallers & MG teams. Coys at disposal OC Coys. Casualties, 4 men wounded 1 man died of wounds.	

Hour, date and place	Summary of events and Information	Remarks & references to appendices
17 Sept.	Batt'n relieved 1st Welch Reg in trenches E of KEMMEL. A B & D Coys holding Fire & support trenches. A Coy in addition holding one supporting point & C Coy holding one supporting point. Remainder C Coy Batt'n reserve at KEMMEL School. All MGs in Fire trenches Bn HQ at DOCTOR'S HOUSE	
18 Sept	Enemy shelled trenches on our right held by B Coy dropping about 50 HE shells 8" calibre between 1.30 pm & 4 pm also 2 HE shells into trenches on our left held by A Coy. Damage 4 bays blown in. Damage repaired at night. Casualties up to 12 noon 1 wounded.	

93

Hour, date and place	Summary of events and Information	Remarks references to appendices
19 Sept cont.	Officers 3rd Canadian Bde guided round trenches for reconnaissance in view of relief night 20/21 Sept. About 3.45 pm enemy shelled trenches on our right held by B Coy dropping about 7 H.E. 8" shells. Three of these landed between 2 shell trenches blowing them in & burying about 12 men six of whom died from effects. Casualties up to 12 noon 1 killed 6 wounded 2 sick from shock.	
20 Sept	Battn relieved in the trenches by 16th Canadian Reg. On relief marched to LOCRE & billeted. Situation during day quiet. Casualties up to 12 noon 6 Killed 21 Wounded 7 Shock these caused by bombardment on 19 Sept.	

94

Hour, date and place	Summary of events and information	Remarks and references to Appendices
21 Sept	Battn marched in Brigade from Locre at 9.0 am to PRADELLE billeting about ROUGE CROIX Arriving 12.30 pm	
22 Sept	Battn at ROUGE CROIX Physical training. Training Bombers, M.G teams, Signallers Coy drill & interior economy	
23 Sept	Battn at ROUGE CROIX. Physical training. Route march. Battn held in readiness to turn out in ½ hour till 6.0 am 24.9.16	
24 Sept	Battn at ROUGE CROIX. Physical training Route march. Practiced telling off in parties & moving from field for en-bussing on main road.	

Hour, date and place	Summary of events and Information	Remarks and references to Appendices
25th Sept.	Battn at ROUGE CROIX. Battn inspected by O.C. 82nd Inf Bde	
26 Sept	Battn marched in Bde from ROUGE CROIX to billets at QUENTIN	
27 Sept	Battn left its billets at QUENTIN & bus-bussed at PARADIS, de-bussed at BETHUNE & marched to billets at SAILLY-~~LABOURE~~ LABOURSE	
28 Sept	Battn in billet at SAILLY-LABOURSE. Coys physical exercise, musketry & training.	
29th Sept	Battalion marched to ANNIQUINN at 3.30 p.m. Stood to arms ½ an hours' notice for the night.	

Date/Place	Summary of events and information	Remarks and references to Appendices
30th	Battalion relieved 9th Lan Regt in the trenches in Big Willie Trench and about 150 yards of Hohenzollern Redoubt on the Left.	
8/10/15	Maxwell Comdg 2/Lancs	Captain 2/Cheshire Regt Fusiliers

84th Bde.
28th Div.

Battalion embarked for Salonika 23.10.15.

2nd NORTHUMBERLAND FUSILIERS.

OCTOBER

1915

On His Majesty's Service.

Hour, date and place.	Summary of events and information	Remarks and references to appendices
1st Oct 15	About dawn an hour after the Battalion had taken over the trenches the enemy, working unobserved down an old communication trench, which ran from their line into the junction of BIG WILLIE and HOHENZOLLERN Redoubt, gained a footing of about 100 yards by a surprise bomb attack. C & D Companies at whose junction this attack took place at once built a double barrier and stopped further advance. About 6 pm C and D boys assisted by a bombing party from 2/Cheshire Regt	

Hour, date and place	Summary of events and information	Remarks and references to appendices
1st Oct continued	(in a sap to the rear) by heavily bombing from right, left and rear, retook about 50 yards of the ground lost.	
2nd	This was repeated several times after but without further success.	
3rd Oct	Between 5 & 6 a.m. the enemy having gained a footing in LITTLE WILLIE (held by 1st WELCH) came rapidly down the trench from left to right bombing their way through 1st Welch & 2nd Cheshire Regt forced D. Coy backward into the barrier. The survivors (26 men) falling back over	

99

Hour, date and place	Summary of events and information	Remarks and references to appendices
3rd Continued	over the open on to the support trench in rear. This bombardment was most violent and the grenades which were very large, were well thrown, came in a constant hail breaking down all resistance and killing all before it. The barrier previously built by C Company stopped any further advance. Capt. Freeman, 9/Cheshire Regt. took command of D Coy ½ an hour before this attack took place, as there were no officers of the Coy. left. Capt Lamb being wounded and	Continued in Book II

1915

Date	Summary of Events	Ref to Appx
3rd Oct Cont'd	and 2/Lieut J.H.L Gilchrist a/adjutant, killed the previous night. The Battalion was relieved by the King's Own Royal Lancaster Regt at 3pm and took up a position in reserve in the control Keep for the night The following casualties occurred among the Officers Lieut. Col. C.A. ARMSTRONG — Killed 1/10/15 Capt. W E JENKINS — Killed 1/10/15 2/Lieut & acting Adjutant J.H.L. GILCHRIST — Killed 2/10/15 Capt. R.M.R. LAMB — Wounded 3/10/15 " R H HOFFMAN — wounded 3/10/15 " F.C. LONGDEN (4D29) — wounded 1/10/15 Lieut. A.J HOPKINSON (4D29) — wounded 1/10/15 2/Lieut H.A FORDHAM — wounded 3/10/15 " G SWEET — wounded 1/10/15 " D F C BACON (4D29) — wounded 2/10/15 " G WILKINS — Wounded 3rd Died 4/10/15 " B. GREW — wounded 1/10/15 " S.A. ROSE — wounded 1/10/15 " H J HOLMES — wounded 1/10/15	VERMELLES.

Date	Summary of Event	Ref to Appx
31st Oct	Officer R.B. Howell (#hon 9th/4) Wounded & Missing	10/15
	Casualties among the men:	
	Killed 2&3 wmd.	
	Missing believed Killed 99/100 bars	
	Wounded 115	
	Missing #6 md	
4th	The Battn took up a position in Lancashire Trenches (Reserve) relieving 2/Cheshire Regt.	
	Capt. E.B. Maxwell 2nd Cheshire Regt took over temporary command	
	No. 4 Coy reformed by withdrawing one platoon from No.1, 2 & 3 Companies.	
	Officer P.S. Johnson (3 DCI) appointed a/adjt.	
5th	Battalion relieved in Lancashire Trenches by the 2nd Bn The Baffs, and marched to Annequin at 10 a.m. & at 6 p.m. marched to Béthune, billets for the night.	

Date	Summary of Events	Ref to Appx.
6th	Battalion marched in Bde at 10 am for BUSNES and billeted at LAGLETTE near BUSNES.	
7th	Battalion resting. Major General S Bulfin visited Battn & complimented it on the good work during last few mths.	
8th	Battalion Training. Bathing and practising Bombing etc. Major B Bogle West York Rgt assumed Command	
9th	Battalion Physical Training. Digging at night. Musketry. Bombing. Coy parades forming up, for digging by day & by night	
10th	Sunday. Physical training. Digging trenches Church parade. Coy drill in afternoon. Instruction in Bombing	
11th	Route March. Major B Cruddas joined from 1st Battalion –	

1915

Date	Summary of Events	Ref. to Appx.
Oct 12th	Training in musketry. Trench Bombing and platoon Bombers instructed in bombing. Coys in close order drill. — Major. W. Bogle left to rejoin his Batt: 2/East Yorks Rgt. — The following officers joined as re-enforcement — Lieut C.R. Freeman 3/Nor 3us " G.V. Fenwick " 2/Lieut H.U. Scrutton " " F.V. Carpenter " " F.A. Price " " G.G. Shiel " " J.C.L. Redwood " " C. Jones " " G.M. Dawe 3/Dorset Rgt	
13th	Bn practised in route marching. Companies inspected by Comdg officer. The following officers joined as re-enforcement:— 2/Lieut Jno Dingle " Clive Smith —	

Date	Summary of Events	Appx.
14th	Battalion engaged in Physical and Company Training	
15th	Battn inspected by the Brigade Commander Weir DSO. and training as on 14th. 2/Lt Gm Dawe 3/Dorset to Hospital	
16th	Battn training as on 14th & 15th. Comdg Officer (Major B Bruddas) visited trenches at Cuinchy	
17th	Battn attended Church Parade. Officers instructed in Lewis Gun mechanism and in Bombing.	
18th	Battn marched to Mont BERNENCHON and was billeted on farms.	
19th	Battn marched to BETHUNE and billeted	

1915

Date	Summary of Events	Appx.
19th	in The Tobacco Factory RUE de LILLE. The Commanding Officer Capt Allgood, 2/Lieut Price and 2/Lt Shiel Machine Gun Officer reconnoitred the Cambrin Support point.	
20	Physical training. Orders received that Batt would ~~avaluavit~~ entrain next day for a place over sea not stated.	
21.	Battalion entrained at Fouquereil station near BETHUNE at 11.30 am and left in one special train at 12.30 pm for MARSEILLES. Strength 21 Officers 697 Men. 71 Horses. Vehicles 19 2nd line vehicles left behind with No 3 Coy Army Service Corps.	

Oct/15

Date	Summary of Events	Ref. to appx.
22	Batt'n en route for MARSEILLES via AMIENS, PARIS, Montereau, Dijon, Lyon, VALENCES.	
23	Batt'n arrived MARSEILLES at 1 P.M. and embarked at 2.30 P.M. in the (Cunard) H.M.T. IVERNIA. 40 Horses embarked in H.M.T. SHROP-SHIRE in charge of 2nd Lt H E Gardner. Other Units on board Brigade Staff (84th) 1st Suffolk Reg't & 2nd Cheshire Reg't.	

The following Officers embarked in H.M.T IVERNIA
Major B Cruddas Comdg.
Capt+Q'M' N M Allan
2/Lieut P R Johnston a/adjt 4/DCI
Chaplain Capt T A Royce.
M Officer Lieut H Bourne Taylor. RAMC
M.G.O 2/Lieut G G Shiel
No 1 Coy (A)
  Lieut D J Allgood
  2/Lieut T C L Redwood

23rd Cont?	2/Lieut K.A. Woodroffe No 2 Coy (B) Lieut G.A. Fenwick 2/Lieut C.G. Wright " 7.A. Price " B.C. Woodroffe " Jno Dingle No 3 Coy C Lieut C.K. Freeman 2/Lieut 7.V. Carpenter No 4 Coy D Lieut O. Barr Ellison 2/Lieut H.U. Scrutton " G. Clarke " Clive Smith 4 W.O.' 656 Other Ranks* In the H.M.T. Shropshire 2/Lieut H.T. Gardner + 39 men left at Marseilles to follow 2nd Lt C.A. Steel + 33 men and part of transport.	*Includes 17 Bde Band.
24.	Sailed at 4 pm Destination stated to be SALONIKA.	

Date	Summary of Events.	Ref. to Appx.
25=	Batn at sea - South West of Sardinia at 4-5pm Good passage Lecture by Brigadier Gen at 6pm "General Subject" Physical training morning + afternoon -	
26th	Battalion at sea. Sailing South of Southern Coast of Sicily all morning Good passage Physical training as on 25th. Lecture by Major Needham Div: Staff "Discipline"	
27th	Battalion at Sea Passage rough. Tea 2pm. Lecture 'Advanced Guard' by Major Needham.	
28th	Battalion at Sea Passage fine Physical training as usual.	

Date		
28th	Lecture "Outpost" by Major Winston Olivr Div: Staff	
29th	H.M.T. "Ivernia" anchored in harbour at Alexandria at 4 am. Training as usual. Advance party 1 Officer + 30 men proceeded to Mamourah Camp at 1.30 pm to prepare Camp	
30th	Battalion disembarked at 9 + noon - & proceeded in two trains from Alexandria to Mamourah Camp. Weather hot	
31st	Church Parade. Preliminary instruction by Commanders of Companies. Weather hot	

J B Cuddy Major
Comdg 2/ nrnh 5 Fus

www.ingramcontent.com/pod-product-compliance
Lightning Source LLC
Chambersburg PA
CBHW081546160426
43191CB00011B/1849